D0895066

Hello Friends!

Places I Know

Imagine That!

Oh, What Fun!

Let's Go Outside

What a Funny Animal!

IMAGINATION
An Odyssey Through Language

What a
Funny Animal!

Gail Heald-Taylor
General Consultant, Language Arts

HBJ **HARCOURT BRACE JOVANOVICH, PUBLISHERS**

Orlando   San Diego   Chicago   Dallas

Acknowledgments

For permission to reprint copyrighted material, grateful acknowledgment is made to the following sources:

Greenwillow Books, a division of William Morrow & Company, Inc.: Have You Seen My Duckling?, written and illustrated by Nancy Tafuri. Copyright © 1984 by Nancy Tafuri.

Harper & Row, Publishers, Inc.: Do You Want To Be My Friend? by Eric Carle. Published by Thomas Y. Crowell, 1971 and protected by the Berne Convention. All rights reserved.

Bobbi Katz: From "Company" (Retitled: "Lunch for a Dinosaur") in *Upside Down and Inside Out: Poems for All Your Pockets* by Bobbi Katz. Copyright © 1973 by Bobbi Katz.

Hal Leonard Publishing Corporation: "Barnyard Song" from *Songs to Grow On,* edited by Beatrice Landeck. Copyright © 1950 by Edward B. Marks Music Corporation; copyright renewed. All rights reserved.

Macmillan Publishing Company: "A Bear Went Over the Mountain" from *THE ROOSTER CROWS: A Book of American Rhymes and Jingles* by Maud and Miska Petersham. Copyright 1945 by Macmillan Publishing Company, renewed 1973 by Miska F. Petersham.

Art Credits

Eric Carle: 48-76; Marie-Louise Gay: 34-39, 46, 47; Sharon Harker: 30-31; Tony Kenyon: 28, 29, 32, 33; Nancy Schill: 40-45; Nancy Tafuri: 2-27

Cover: Tom Vroman

Contents

Have You Seen My Duckling?

A story by Nancy Tafuri

Early one morning...

6

Have you seen my duckling?

12

13

Have you seen my duckling?

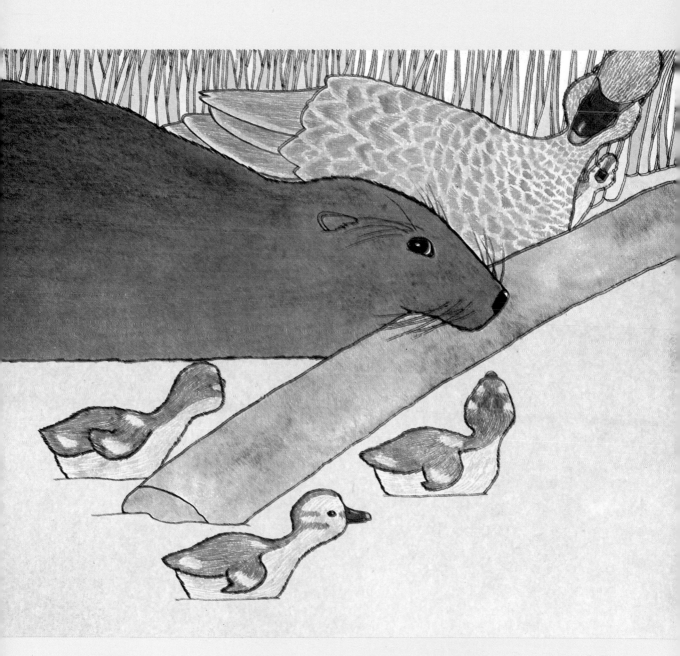

Have you seen my duckling?

Have you seen my duckling?

Have you seen my duckling?

21

27

To Market, To Market

A Mother Goose rhyme

To market, to market,
  To buy a fat pig,
Home again, home again,
  Jiggety-jig.
To market, to market,
  To buy a fat hog,
Home again, home again,
  Jiggety-jog.

Picture by Tony Kenyon

Hickory, Dickory, Dock

A Mother Goose Rhyme

Hickory, dickory, dock,
The mouse ran up the clock.
　　The clock struck one.
　　The mouse ran down,
Hickory, dickory, dock.

Picture by Sharon Harker

31

Higglety, Pigglety, Pop

An old rhyme

Higglety, pigglety, pop!
The dog has eaten the mop;
The pig's in a hurry,
The cat's in a flurry,

Higglety, piggelty,

POP!

33

Barnyard Song

A Kentucky folk song

I had a cat, and the cat pleased me,

I fed my cat under yonder tree.

Cat goes fiddle dee dee.

Pictures by Marie-Louise Gay

I had a hen, and the hen pleased me,
I fed my hen under yonder tree.
Hen goes chimmy chuck, chimmy chuck,
Cat goes fiddle dee dee.

35

I had a duck, and the duck pleased me,
I fed my duck under yonder tree.
Duck goes quack, quack,
Hen goes chimmy chuck, chimmy chuck,
Cat goes fiddle dee dee.

I had a cow, and the cow pleased me,

I fed my cow under yonder tree.

Cow goes moo, moo,

Duck goes quack, quack,

Hen goes chimmy chuck, chimmy chuck,

Cat goes fiddle dee dee.

38

Connections

A Zookeeper at Work

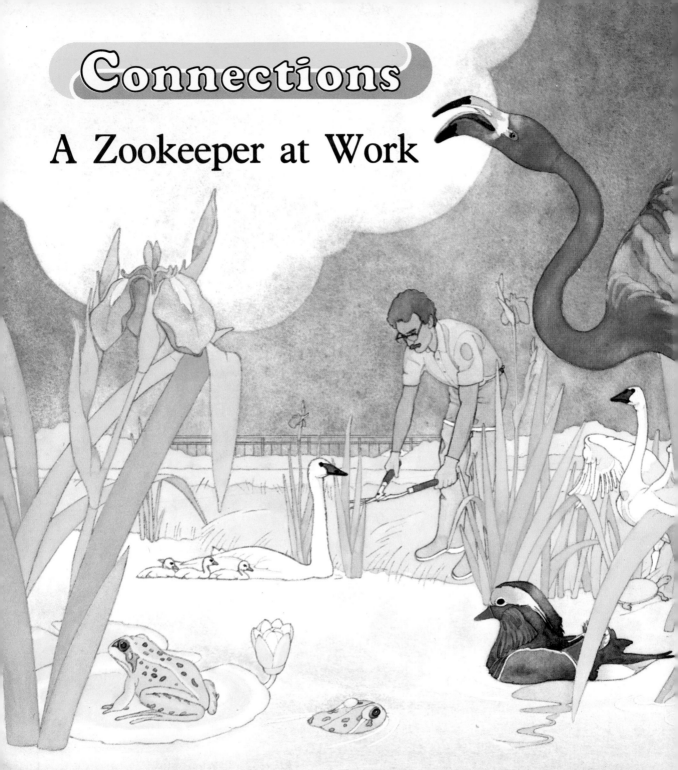

A zookeeper works in the zoo.

The monkeys are hungry.
What does the zookeeper do?

The elephant needs a bath.

What do the zookeepers do?

There is a new baby giraffe.

What does the zookeeper do?

Children visit the zoo.

What do the zookeepers do?

A Bear Went Over the Mountain

An American folk rhyme

A bear went over the mountain,
A bear went over the mountain,
A bear went over the mountain
To see what he could see.

The other side of the mountain,
The other side of the mountain,
The other side of the mountain
Was all that he could see!

Lunch for a Dinosaur

From the poem "Company" by Bobbi Katz

I'm fixing a lunch for a dinosaur.
Who knows when one might come by?
I'm pulling up all the weeds I can find.
I'm piling them high as the sky.
I'm fixing a lunch for a dinosaur.
I hope he will stop by soon.
Maybe he'll just walk down my street
And have some lunch at noon.

Pictures by Marie-Louise Gay

Do You Want To Be My Friend?

A story by Eric Carle

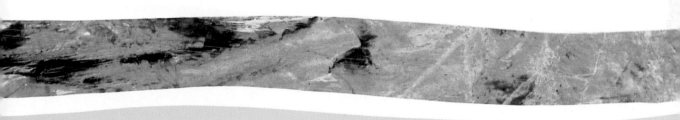

60

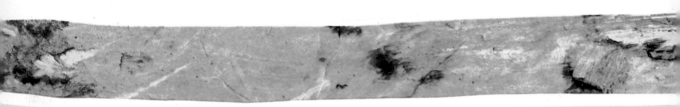

64

71